For The People To Drink

For The People To Drink

Erika Kimberly Stanley

EK Book Publishing

dedication

Dad, Mom, & Ellis, this and everything I do is a love offering for you.

EK Book Publishing
Bridgeport, CT
www.EKbookpublishing.com
writer@erikakimberly.com

ISBN: 978-0-578-62870-7

Trade Distribution:
In the US. EK Book Publishing. www.EKbookpublishing.com

Cover Photography & Graphic Design by Erika K. Stanley

Interior photographs by Erika K.Stanley

10 9 8 7 6 5 4 3 2 1

"The art of losing isn't hard to master;
so many things seem filled with the intent
to be lost that their loss is no disaster."

-Elizabeth Bishop, One Art[1]

contents

This book really started

when I was in second grade.

I had been accepted into High Horizons Magnet School the year before, you know on a lottery, and my teacher from first grade, Mrs. Felberbaum, moved up to teach second grade. Somewhere between playing with duck scissors, peeling myself out of a purple snow suit during Winter, and making new friends I learned what it meant to be an author. One day, Mrs. Felerbaum had the class sit on a circle carpet when a guest speaker from Fairfield talked to us about her life as an author. She passed around copies of her book and I remember, even now, the voice inside my head that said "I want to be a writer, too."

In third grade, I wrote my first haiku while the rest of the class played with toys and one another. I was captivated with words and manipulating them on the page, and to me, that was fun, more fun than whatever games my classmates were playing. During those years, the Bridgeport Public School system had a Young Author's program, a youth writing, editing, and book binding competition, and I won first place TWICE. My mom and I went to UB (the University of Bridgeport) and I remember looking at her from that huge stage feeling like the world's greatest.

From reciting Robert Frost and Shakespeare to changing my major in college to English to scribbling poems on Filenes receipt paper, this book started years ago. I wrote it and lived it simultaneously. I've carried this book with me from the moment I became aware of the awesome details of my life; those memories are written inside of me forever.

Erika Kimberly

1

prelude

Inside the cracks of concrete roads
Between streetlights dimly lit
Wrapped around traffic jams
Beneath factory stacks with chipped paint
A city, long forgotten sits on the Sound.
Bridgeport, Connecticut.
The largest city in the state.
They say we have the smallest amount of hope
Yet here, the sun still shines.
Maybe this is God's way of giving second
and third chances.
But will anyone ever look
Up to the sky
Raise their open palms
And take from God
The manna of this morning.

Seventh Floor
Bridgeport Hospital

What's That Sound?

27A

There is no "B" to follow
miss this exit
and you can still sneak
your way in. Bridgeport—
city of illusions

everywhere, everyone knows
there are more
ways to get in, than
to get out.
Around the bend

this highway will dump
you downtown
but what's that sound?
Drums and hums, electricity
shoots through wires.

Sign says "Welcome to the Park City"
Silver slabs support
Brick laid on brick
Busted bumpy roads
Cans clogged with trash, Bridgeport—

city of confusion. Where
Are you looking to go?
What are you looking
For? Here, you'll find
Everything and nothing

At the same time.
Pick a street, a corner
That intersects with another
And you'll see
What used to be, the history
That now hangs
in the balance.

hometown glory

I'm from the lip of wet ceilings
discolored walls and chipped Cadillacs.

I'm from busted street lights
rusty love affairs, and saggy power lines.

I'm from the bodega behind the fence
decorated in trash.

I'm from the screams of dripped graffiti
corrupt campaigns, and Malt liquor tears.

I'm from empty trust funds
shoebox bank accounts, and Master degrees in street smarts.

I'm from faded henna, spanglish
and the rough edges of patwa.

I'm from Grandma's earthly cheek
and the creak, in Grandfather's tin lunch box.

I'm from the cooking oil's jive
on Soul Food Sunday.

I'm from blazing bullet wounds
"Gone too soon" pins and "girl, remember when?"

I'm from soup kitchens
boarded up museums, and fenced in playgrounds.

I'm from the place where Jesus
is always on the main line, but few really call Him.

I'm from where you don't
make wishes on shooting stars

You say prayers to the flashes
on ambulances and sirens of cop cars.

the pull

Pot holes swallow
the left tire
of my new car. I grip
the wheel
to fight the natural
pull of the city—
This place, always tries
to take people
where they don't
want to go.

aftermath

Superstorm Sandy hit Bridgeport,CT in 2012 and wreaked havoc on the shoreline city.

Down a side street, brown speckles of fragmented rock scatter.

Resting on the side of the road is a rusty red Chevrolet truck.

Over the wheel, water swims, as the rest of the truck leans sloppily to the right.

Where is the owner?

No sign of him anywhere.

Inching down the street, more water. Where are the people?

No one is here to witness this disaster with me.

Guessing, I think, is this the effect of a superstorm or is this is everyday life?

preying on those who pray

Venomous flames crack
Devilish black smoke aims high —
a peace offering.

how I learned social studies

Best storyteller in Bridgeport,
my father is. Every time we wiz
through streets, he taps the window
"that's where we bought
hamburgers for 15 cents". He,
like me, holds this city in his heart.

I didn't have to sit restlessly
in a class to learn the curves
of the road that turn you around
and get you off balance. No geography.
I learned by the curves around
my father's fingers that point
into the air like a laser
with the power to cut through time

to remind me what was, really still is,
when we get underneath it all.

the voice of democracy

It's faint. Slow to rise like clouds
hovering the Sound in Early August.
Hundreds of thousands mummer
and I feel it pulse around me. Am I
the only one who hears them? Lift

the hood of a 2003 Honda Civic parked
on East Main Street. Pull back
the dusted curtain of Astoria Park's
oldest room. Turn the corner
into Marina Village, there behind
the playground, out of the mouths
of babes it hangs in mid-air

a catching for the wind.
It is the thing brushing our bare
arms in Summer. A mist to us
in Winter, a puffed up vapor
as it rises up to God.
It is a cracked voice.

Now? Do you hear it?

No History

the Greatest Show

Before he went under the bloodshot
and canary colored tent, there was already
     a spectacle.
Before any flames were swallowed up
by hungry bellies and before dumbos
ever took flight, Joice Heath was Barnum's
first attraction. "unquestionably the most
astonishing and interesting curiosity
in   the   world."

Nine to nine, three to five, six to ten
onlookers staggered up the hotel stairs
carouseled around the old nurse
watching the grey clouds fill her eyes
and the wrinkles, thick dark, and leather-like
were a map taking each of them nowhere
that can be found from here.

Perched up in a bed of sorrows
she whispered songs to the beating echo
of African hills, this is what kept her
alive now. The 46 pounds of a woman
used to wipe, dress, and nurse
the man called "our Founding Father".

But what is a father without a mother?
The birth of a nation began
not in Joice's womb, but in her arms.
And you know, that kid, walking down Washington
Avenue doesn't know that this
is   his   history.

that the Greatest Show was nothing
without the "original, authentic and indisputable"
Black mother of a white son.
He'd think it was a joke. And that's the thing
about jesting — at some point it's
just   not   funny.

THE GREATEST
Natural & National
CURIOSITY
IN THE WORLD.

JOICE HETH,

Nurse to Gen. GEORGE WASHINGTON, (the Father of our Country,)
WILL BE SEEN AT

Barnum's Hotel, Bridgeport,

On FRIDAY, and SATURDAY, the 11th, & 12th days
of December, DAY and EVENING.

also Monday

JOICE HETH is unquestionably the most astonishing and interesting curiosity in the World! She was the slave of Augustine Washington, (the father of Gen. Washington,) and was the first person who put clothes on the unconscious infant, who, in after days, led our heroic fathers on to glory, to victory, and freedom. To use her own language when speaking of the illustrious Father of his Country, "she raised him." JOICE HETH was born in the year 1674, and has, consequently, now arrived at the astonishing

AGE OF 161 YEARS.

She Weighs but FORTY-SIX POUNDS, and yet is very cheerful and interesting. She retains her faculties in an unparalleled degree, converses freely, sings numerous hymns, relates many interesting anecdotes of *the boy* Washington, and often laughs heartily at her own remarks, or those of the spectators. Her health is perfectly good, and her appearance very neat. She is a baptist and takes great pleasure in conversing with ministers and religious persons. The appearance of this marvellous relic of antiquity strikes the beholder with amazement, and convinces him that his eyes are resting on the oldest specimen of mortality they ever before beheld. Original, authentic, and indisputable documents accompanying her prove, however astonishing the fact may appear, that JOICE HETH is in every respect the person she is represented.

The most eminent physicians and intelligent men in Cincinnati, Philadelphia, New-York, Boston, and other places, have examined this *living skeleton* and the documents accompanying her, and all, *invariably*, pronounce her to be, as represented, 161 *years of age!*

A female is in continual attendance, and will give every attention to the ladies who visit this relic of by-gone ages.

She has been visited in Philadelphia, New-York, Boston, &c., by more than TWENTY THOUSAND Ladies and Gentlemen, within the last three months.

Hours of Exhibition, from 9 A. M. to 1 P. M. and from 3 to 5, and 6½ to 10 P. M.

ADMITTANCE 25 Cents, CHILDREN HALF-PRICE.

Printed by J. BOOTH & SON, 147, Fulton-st N. Y.

Remains Monday the 14th

Sonnet 1883

In 1883, the Bridgeport & Port Jefferson Steam Boat Company was created. The ferry company still sails from Bridgport, CT to Port Jefferson, Long Island today.

miles and miles, sailing through the in-between
miles and miles, sailing through the in-between
miles and miles, sailing through the in-between
miles and miles, sailing through the in-between

miles and miles, sailing through the in-between
miles and miles, sailing through the in-between
miles and miles, sailing through the in-between
miles and miles, sailing through the in-between

miles and miles, sailing through the in-between
miles and miles, sailing through the in-between
miles and miles, sailing through the in-between
miles and miles, sailing through the in-between

miles and miles, sailing through the in-between
miles and miles, sailing through the in-between

the Subway[*]

"Appetite, an universal wolf"- Trolius & Cressida, William Shakespeare

We all hunger — trapped inside
hollow passages we travel alone,
possibilities endless
as we move up and down
our colorless, genderless selves.
Gonging sound, the pangs
echo into bleak blackness.

We all thirst — throats parched
whispers lost in still air of hope,
lips crack. We mouth for
morsels of water to cool our
desperate longings when the engine
shakes us almost dry.

For most of us, it is this craved
crazed side of us that keeps us alive.

They too hunger —helplessly
unable to chisel out of tunnels
they've traveled through year
after year. Grit beneath nails
their desperation evident.

Who is to blame? You?
Me? Them? What if
instead of blame,
we've been sent to pluck
pieces from our loaves
to fill the inner man

whose outer man's hand
reaches for yours. The crumbs
they seek rots in our bread boxes
and baskets. They want what
they do not have. We have
what we do not give.
We all hunger. We all thirst.

*Subway Restaurant was founded in Bridgeport, CT in 1965.

Zuri's Bookstore

On Saturdays, we'd go to that world
of books - it felt H U G E
in space, but really
it was massive in content, deep dark and lovely
like us. My parents, my brother, and me
would climb out our Copper colored Vista
and walk into the bookstore
Black and proud.

There, I would flip through Eloise Greenfield
books about black girls who looked
like me, kinky hair lustrous and detangled
my own smelling like Pink lotion.
My brother always found his way
thumbing through basketball books
or searching for Black heros.

My first Kwanzaa celebration
was there - a man beat an African drum
a lady sung and her voice rung words
I can't remember but that feeling
of Blackness bore itself heavy
all over me. I was Black and proud
in the heart of the city - Bridgeport -
and there was nothing better than
the way Zuri's bookstore gave us
a home within a home.

remind me to tell you about Remington

Frosted and aged windows cloud
facts we search endlessly for
when we drive, walk
down city streets and ask
how long has this been here? Or
what is this?

Outside — shabby concrete foundations
kicked away by time, wilted weeds weave
stories I've heard
once, twice, or more. This history
never felt like history
in the making, but what ever does?

Ammunition shot through shipments
from this factory. Sales slid past desks
for years. And who cared
about what the future
would bring?

This history, a shadow of what
we live in. Ammunition now shooting
through Fairfield Avenue and Main
Street. Watch out!
Fragments of the past
will shoot you and you won't
be able to see
what that little boy
or his sister could be
if Remington never came to take
what was growing, right here
in this city.

You're Out!

Drive by the Bridgeport Bluefish stadium, and it's still there, but the Bridgeport Bluefish aren't up to bat. What's sad is I used to love to watch a game with my feet up on the chair in front of me screaming for the guys in uniform to "run!" But somewhere there was a boy in the city who wasn't at the game and running from the cops. Fear beating in his chest, but the natural instinct inside drove him to run home.

That's what's been happening. Our kids are on the run. Bluefish, ball games, baseball. None of that changes the real-life struggles of our youth. They're stuck between bases - the corner and trying to get back home - and I'm cheering for every one of them. You should, too, because this is real life, and real-life is not a game. There are wins and losses, but those losses mean someone ends up in a pine box or trapped in a cage.

One strike, two strike, three and you're out!

Instead of the crowd, the streets are going wild.

No Escape

In 2009, a fire inside an apartment unit of the P.T. Barnum public housing complex killed a young woman and her three children.

Hammering at the door

echoes down the hallway

thicks puffs of clouds

licked up all that good air

the stairs were mountainous

he could not come down

and at the same time love lay

at the door and she couldn't

answer it - that single entry door

gave no way out

the angel of death lurking

some said intoxication

others said forgetfulness

I say, the city failed you.

This History

Pretty Girl

First girl in elementary school to wear lipstick
We envied her.
Eyes painted like our dolls, hips round
like our mothers,
her voice never cracked.

She knew we were in awe
       For what child carries
Confidence instead
       Of books to class?
Pretty girl, storyteller
       We were her audience.
She was twelve,
       Tongue wagging
In the sweaty air of gym class
       To show us still
Blinded by innocence
       How to "kiss a boy like you mean it".

Pretty girl no one told you
The God honest truth.
Being pretty
Comes with a price.
And being pretty
Doesn't pay enough
To pick up the tab.

ways of womanhood

I.

Was it impossible to think—
To drum up dreams in the distant future
And find my silhouette
Dancing in the wind?
Or were there moments
In the minutes that unfolded in your life
Where you saw me, clearly, and knew
From your womb a seed would grow
Into a tree with fruits and flowers
I would resemble?

II.

I know the terrain —
The height in my cheekbones
Are mountains on sienna shaded flat plains
That blend seamlessly into every woman before
Me. When happiness spills out
Uncontrollably rushing like ocean waves
Of the deep tides
Bringing in stories of way back then
They merge with the currents of my mine.
I am the joy they stole and thought
We would never ever, ever find again
But I rise like the tide at Seaside.

III.

When the article emerged in the New York Times
About one in every six teenage girls
Becoming a single parent
Was no one here was reading it?
Were most girls sitting at their window
Like a caged bird
Stung by the harsh awkward cusp
Of a child body betraying and a
womanly body coming too soon?
Words of the future no one warned them about.
A future that clipped so many wings before
Anyone could notice.

But I,
In my own awkward years
Would tightrope between
The child of my past
And the woman of my future,
Find and flap my wings

And fly.

my child

To the foster children from every city in Connecticut

Does the red shade in this dress make you blue?
Is it too bright? Too bold like the darkness
you were taken out of? I try,
to use every seed of premature maternal instinct
but are you happy in a world that has flung
so much dirt on you?

Do you remember the room we gave to you,
spilling over with teddy bears, books, a dollhouse,
dressers filled with wonderfully pink things?
You wanted new shoes, new red ones "like Erika's?"
And stung by the sharpness in your gaze I bought them,
didn't I? I dressed you like a porcelain doll, cracked
yet not fully broken.

Wasn't I creating a hope in you
when I laid beside your bed
and read stories to give you an escape
from the ones you knew about fighting
between your mother and men
who were not your father.
Didn't I teach you to use your hands for prayer
instead of hitting your classmates
but it was so hard for you to understand.

Didn't I give you my smile, mornings when I rose
early to peek at your still face
and on evenings I inched up the steps,
never wanting to wake you,
but you would jump eagerly from behind the door
because you were waiting for me?

All this and now my child you do not smile?
Are you afraid I do not love you?
Do you fear I will shatter you, disappoint you,
leave you destitute, vacant
like a city that has lost its glory?
Haven't I tried to mend the broken
memories you cling to?
But I question now,
will my hands work fast enough?
And will you, before you are plucked from my life,
if for no one else smile for me?

beside betrayal

In an abandoned bowl
creamy pancake mix bubbles in irritation,
the orange message indicator flashes
from the computer screen,
a caution I did not heed.
Cell phone rings
buried alive
beneath books in a bag by the door.
I threw it when news
came through the speaker
minutes before.
Now, I feel like a child, in a queen size bed.
Fistfuls of down comforter ooze
out of my grasp. I weep alone in this apartment.
Legs kick against the limitless air
my lungs can barely take in,
I want to be free
of this pain, of this moment
but I am shocked by the coldness
in this world.

Would it have felt any different,
hearing the death of you-
if it weren't revealed to me
in morning?
Could I have delayed
the news if night had lasted a little longer,
and slid slowly
back into the hands of God?

Under the dim eye of night
Miles away I couldn't see

when the latches on your back door broke
when men in black hoodies gathered
or when gunshots welcomed you home.
It was in that moment,
the city we both loved betrayed us.
The blast of each searing bullet launched
into the warmth of your youthful flesh
and smoke's broken wings flapped
away from the blazing barrel, high
higher and higher still.

The only promise you ever broke
was "I'll see you soon."
Soon, I found out, would never come.
The weight of this
is chiseled into a chip on my shoulder.
I left my apartment, days later
without ever making those pancakes.
They, at the hand of one of my roommates
were poured down the drain.

Sociology 225: Society and the Individual

Skipped class. The brick wall held me
You know, that one that wraps around
Sides of the university library.
A small opening fixed in the middle
Narrow, but wide enough
For me to fall through.

Slung over my shoulder, a backpack filled
With wrinkled letters. The loyalty she, my best
Friend would have for me. We understood
I would get an education for us.
But instead of writing note cards,
Color coordinating theories to their founders
I found myself reading, rereading
Every letter, line, and phrase she wrote to me.

What could a professor teach me
Outlines sprawled across a whiteboard
When he knew nothing
About shattered dreams of kids who die
In my city? How could he explain
Textbooks penned by men who never experienced
The way life silently hurried by
Me without questioning my stuttering steps?
Why would he test me
When I was the question and the answer,
The theory and the fact?

I rose, I shifted the backpack
Walked pass the building of my class.
Through death
I had learned all I needed to know.

The Park City

Sit down here with me. I know you're busy, just stay.
Easy living? We've never really known it, but sit
Awhile and take this in. The view —
Sometimes we forget it's here. Life pulls us
In every direction but back to this bench.
Don't mind the graffiti, it's a love mark.
Everyone leaves one somewhere.

Perhaps God leaves His in the sky as clouds
And we see them to remember we all need to cool off.
Really? I don't know how graffiti and clouds all go together,
Knees bent down tonight, I'll just be thankful for once we got to sit.

The Intersection

Bridgeport isn't like New Haven. Most of our intersections have four-way stop signs. Growing up here, that was normal to me, and I always knew the person to the right of the stop sign has the right-of-way. I think I knew this because I'm observant, but I'd be lying if I said I didn't hear my Dad say that once or twice. My point is, every place I've ever been, every city and town has its way of dividing up the land. That division, those invisible lines we find ourselves entangled in, cut through land and water and they divide our history, too.

In some ways, Bridgeport is the perfect case study for the opportunity gap that plagues Connecticut at large. Now, everyone is talking about how CT is the second most segregated state in the country, but I'm sure if you're from Bridgeport, you've already known that to be true. Without data points and metrics, you've still been able to understand how Main Street looks like four or five different cities depending on which side street you enter in on. The Board of Education has been fighting for state funds since the integration of Black students in the sixties. The state began defunding the schools as they diversified. It's true. I spent hours at the Bridgeport Public Library's History Center researching every CT Post clipping about Central High School from 1950 to 2018, and I learned that the mixed-up outcomes of kids in the city have not been by chance. The intersection of policy and practice and family history and where you live is how we all emerged out of these complexities.

Bridgeport is a map of mixed histories, highways looping lives together, and roadways cutting through opportunities street by street.

right now

waves of change are crashing
the rock wall at Seaside —
don't get lost. Keep your shadow
close. The way back home won't
always be the same as it was yesterday.

mic drop

picture four year old me
coco chubby cheeks
standing on a stool
so I could reach the sink,
collard greens in a salt pool
my tiny hands rubbing leaf to leaf
a cleansing. When I got brave
I looked over my
right shoulder to announce
my hands are cold Grandma
don't you know she said
it's alright baby, you'll be fine.

I was raised to be a woman
I was raised to be strong

to endure the pain
because sometimes what you gain
tastes so so good
like those collard greens
I cooked for the first time
in my new apartment
they tasted like the ancestors.
each bite called up the women
before me - what glory!

and I thought to myself, splashing
Red Hot on the pile of greens,
if Esau's blood cried out to God
I wonder if the soul of Black
women waft as steam
when neck bones on the stove

are dancing the night away.

I hope they are proud of me
because I stole freedom
from a country that never
intended to give it to me.
proud because

no man can rule me.
no man can tame me.

I can't be broken, not even
that one time I was down
on my knees
begging my mother to move her feet,
days after back surgery, down that long
long hallway on the 7th floor
of Bridgeport Hospital

I was so scared.

But if that didn't break me, nothing will
because I will her strength into me
because I was raised by a woman
who was raised by a woman
who was raised to be a woman.

Don't you know my mother's maiden name
is Best?
So, when I tell you I was born for this
I'm not even lying.

more water

It is impossible to live longer than three to four days without water. Our bodies need water to nourish our brains and our organs. I heard somewhere that our heart becomes brittle when we don't drink proper amounts of water. I have no idea if that is true or not, but I want to believe it as my truth because it would make sense for water and for other things I find essential.

I've always needed stories the way our bodies need water. My heart goes dry every time I'm not telling, writing, or listening to a story. When I began writing these poems as a graduate student at Manhattanville College's Master of Fine Arts program, my classmates called them the "Bridgeport poems." and they were. But, more than Bridgeport poems, they were sips of life in a time where I was homesick in such an untraditional way. What no one told me growing up is that survivor's guilt can marry loneliness and produce the feeling of homesickness and make your heart a place you barely recognize.

Writing about Bridgeport saved me when I missed childhood friends and relatives who had died and when I was haunted by dreams of my childhood home only to wake up in a new house, the one my parents built in the suburbs, and at a time in my life when I was reassessing who I was and how I was. Questioning everything through art and language inspired me and quenched my thirst for memories of people and things that rooted and grounded me as a person.

For The People To Drink took me on a journey around my hometown as a writer and scholar. The landscape of home looks a lot different when you're approaching it to unearth the root causes to many of the challenges you've faced or the histories no one talks about that have affected the outcomes in your life. I hope that if you're from Bridgeport, you can find a piece of your history in these pages, and if you're not from Bridgeport, I hope you think about where you are from and how your story intersects with the history of your hometown.

The title For The People To Drink comes from Exodus chapter 17, verses five through six. I randomly read these verses in 2013 when I was finalizing the first draft of this manuscript, and it was perfect for the theme of this book.

And the Lord said to Moses, "Walk on ahead of the people and take some of the elders of Israel with you. Take along in your hand the staff with which you struck the Nile, and go. Behold, I will stand there before you by the rock at Horeb; when you strike the rock, water will come out of it for the people to drink." [2]

I hope this book gave you something to savor.

Erika Kimberly

photo credit

endnotes

1   From The Complete Poems 1927-1979 by Elizabeth Bishop, published by Farrar, Straus & Giroux, Inc. Copyright © 1979, 1983 by Alice Helen Methfessel. Used with permission of Farrar, Straus & Giroux, LLC. All rights reserved.

2   The Holy Bible, New International Version. Grand Rapids: Zondervan House, 1984. Print.

about EK Book Publishing

EK Book Publishing is a cutting edge independent book publisher of fiction, nonfiction, essay, poetry, and mixed-genre work based in Bridgeport, CT. Our stories amplify community voice, social change, and insert fresh discourse into diverse audiences.

about the author

Erika Kimberly Stanley earned a Bachelor of Arts degree in English from the University of Connecticut and a Master of Fine Arts degree in Creative Writing from Manhattanville College. She is the former Editor of the Manhattanville Review and INKWELL literary journal. She's the 2014 Manhattanville Writing Alumni Contest winner. She has facilitated community-based creative writing workshops for PEN America, Minds and Motion, the Wakeman's Boys and Girls Club, and the Brazilian Immigrant Center. Currently, Erika is pursuing a Doctorate of Education degree in Organizational Leadership.

Erika Kimberly Stanley is an author and community educator who writes through the lens of social justice, gender equity, and faith. Erika captures and elevates community voice through creativity and community engagement. She is the creator and host of "Show of Hands," a podcast elevating youth voice in urban spaces. Erika is also the founder of Motifs and Metaphors, a creative writing collective based in Bridgeport.